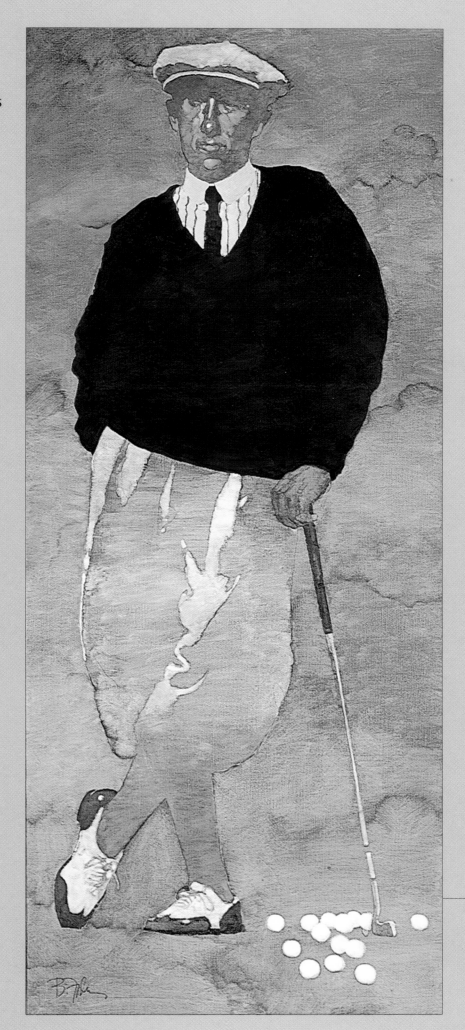

1990
"THE GOLFER"
OIL ON CANVAS

1995
"FLY-FISHING"
OIL ON CANVAS

THE SPORTS ART OF
BART FORBES

Copyright©1998 by Dr. James Beckett

All rights reserved under International and Pan-American
Copyright Conventions.

Published by: Beckett Publications

15850 Dallas Parkway

Dallas, TX 75248

ISBN: 1-887432-51-5

This book was published in association with Bart Forbes.

The staff of Beckett Publications would like to thank

Mr. Forbes for his time and complete cooperation.

First Edition: October 1998

Beckett Corporate Sales and Information (972) 991-6657

1990
"SUPER BOWL III"
OIL ON CANVAS

CONTENTS

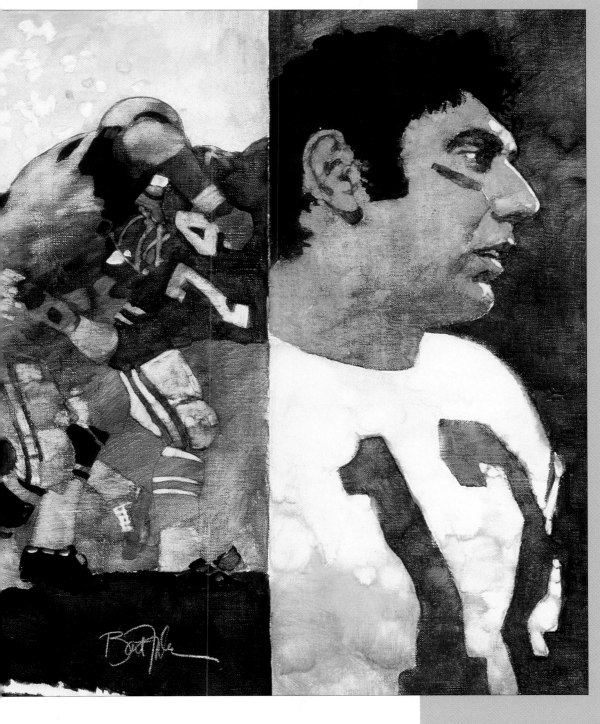

BRUSH
WITH
GREATNESS

From blank canvas to sports artist extraordinaire,

here's your chance to know the work

(and life) of Bart Forbes

Bart Forbes still considers himself more the golfing type than a boxer.

But when you're a young artist looking for a break . . . hey, you do what you have to do.

So Forbes stood in an office throwing imaginary punches, sparring with a writer for a major magazine, trying to get a visual feel for the most famous boxer ever. The resulting artwork, which depicted Muhammad Ali fighting Larry Holmes for a story that would run in Sports Illustrated *before* the 1980 fight, was Forbes' big break. It allowed him to do more of what he enjoys most, and since then, all he's done is become one of the nation's best-known sports artists.

But Forbes is still just a sports guy at heart. A life-long Cincinnati Reds fan, he can still appreciate the unmistakable aura of a baseball game, or the unique pace of a round of golf.

"Probably the only thing that I'd rather do than

This is a painting I did for use as a poster for a lithographer in Chicago. This was a case of creating a generic current-day situation.

I've always been fascinated with the work that catchers have to do. I believe it's the toughest job on the field. I've always been interested in how a catcher calls a game and all the responsibilities he has. He's sort of the choreographer behind the plate.

I worked for a number of years in watercolor exclusively. Some time back I was asked to do some very large paintings, but they were too large to do in watercolor. I had to go to a different medium that I could handle in a smaller size such as 4 by 6 inches. I chose oil and found as I started painting, I could do things that I couldn't with watercolors. Now, probably 90 percent of what I do is oil on canvas or oil on board.

1985
"FASTBALL"
WATERCOLOR

LEFTY GROVE
1926

1995
"LEFTY GROVE"
OIL ON CANVAS

"I'M PARTICULARLY FASCINATED BY THE EARLY PLAYERS IN BASEBALL. GROVE HAD A WONDERFULLY GREAT LOOK ABOUT HIM."

In the "Chief Bender" painting, the character and the uniform are both very appealing to me. "Rube" is based on an early photo of Rube Waddell. It's part of a series I did on early baseball pitchers. "The Hurler" is a generic pitcher (actually based on Stanley Coveleski) that was reproduced as part of a poster series of athletes from that period (the late 1920s). It's sort of an ongoing series. Every now and then I'll add one to it. The paintings in that series are ones that I just do for myself, which is fairly rare for me. Most of the pieces I do are commissioned pieces, but these are personal.

1996
"RUBE"
OIL ON CANVAS

1995
"REGGIE"
OIL ON CANVAS

For a number of years I've collected baseballs with Hall of Famers' signatures on them. One of my favorites is this ball signed by Ty Cobb. I also have a ball signed by Babe Ruth that was a gift from my print publisher.

The painting I did for the Texas Rangers depicts Will Clark at bat. It includes at the top of the painting the home run porch, which helps make The Ballpark such a throwback to the early ballparks.

349^{FT}

325"

Get the real stuff fast.

1994
"FIRST SEASON"
OIL ON CANVAS

1997
"DODGER ICON"
OIL ON CANVAS

These paintings are particularly interesting to me. The first game I saw after I moved to Cincinnati was between the Reds and the Brooklyn Dodgers. The Reds had a pretty mediocre team, but when the Dodgers came to town, you couldn't buy a seat. People were there to see a lot of the great stars, from Hodges to Snider to Campanella.

But I think the person that people were there to see the most was Jackie Robinson. At that time he was playing left field, and I can still remember being there and getting the chance to see someone I had heard so much about. He had two doubles that night and was instrumental in the Dodgers' win. It was something I'll always remember.

In 1997, when I was asked to do these two paintings, I jumped at the chance. It brought back a lot of memories. This is probably one of my favorite assignments. I chose to do the batting scene and the one that says a little bit more about the fact that Jackie was the player that broke the color line.

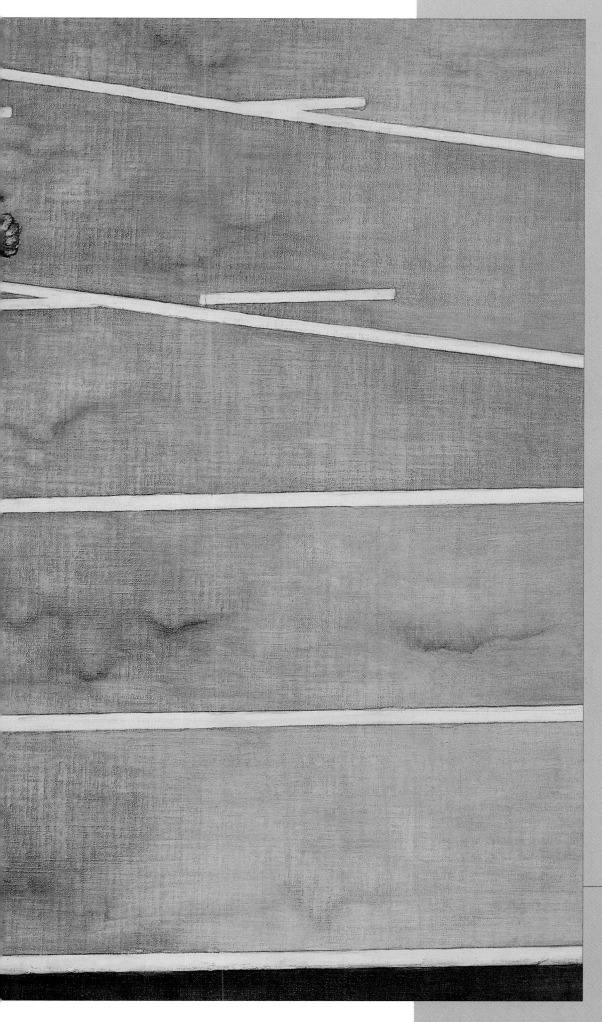

OLYMPICS

I was asked in 1988 by the Korean Olympic Committee to be the official artist for the Seoul Olympics. This involved attending the Games that year and painting a canvas of each Olympic Sport for an Olympic museum in Seoul.

This incredible opportunity took me to Seoul twice. The purpose of the first trip was to become familiar with the city and the Olympic sites, and the second was to attend the Games themselves. I was able to take my wife and our teen-age son and daughter with me. It was a great experience for my family, not only to visit a foreign country, but to have the opportunity to attend the events in and around the Olympic Games.

I intended to spend a lot of time there with my sketchbooks, but when I tried to draw, crowds of curious onlookers would appear, making concentration difficult. So, I resorted to depending upon my camera and telephoto lens and began to shoot as many slides of each event as possible. I ended up with hundreds of images.

After the closing ceremonies, we returned home and I began painting. I completed 26 canvases, based on all the reference slides and sketches in Seoul.

1991
"STARTING LINE"
OIL ON CANVAS

1988
"BALANCE BEAM"
OIL ON CANVAS

SUMMER OLYMPICS

The balance beam piece is typical of many of the paintings I did for the Seoul Games. It's a foreign athlete in a classic pose. Gymnastics was one of the most difficult events to research because the audience was kept at such a distance. Equally difficult were the sailing events in Pusan, a coastal city an hour's plane flight from Seoul. I spent a day on the Sea of Japan in a motorboat with other photographers. It became a great chance to witness sailing events I had never been close to before.

1988
"JACKIE"
OIL ON CANVAS

1988
"FIGHTER"
OIL ON CANVAS

Photo Reference

Photo Reference

The "Fighter" isn't so much a portrait as it is a character study. I like the headgear and the look of the boxer's face. This is one that I didn't want to be an action scene. He had a sort of attitude about him that was very appealing.

1988
"SEOUL RUNNERS"
GRAPHITE

RUNNERS - SEOUL 1988

T hese are typical of the sports I had never seen before the Seoul Games. The Tae Kwon Do match drew a great deal of interest, as did the judo event. These are very big sports in the Orient. The crowds were huge, there were cheerleaders, electric megaphones and all sorts of music.

Photo Reference

1988
"WELTERWEIGHTS"
OIL ON CANVAS

1988
"JUDO BREAK"
OIL ON CANVAS

1988
"GOLD, SILVER AND
BRONZE"
OIL ON CANVAS

1988
"AFTER THE TURN"
OIL ON CANVAS

"**G**old, Silver and Bronze" was actually done for the 1991 Goodwill Games in Seattle. I was asked to do a painting for a poster that would depict the three levels of medal competition. I chose a women's swimming event and positioned the three winners.

In "After the Turn," I wanted to get an underwater effect, so I used a shot of a diver going into the water and then developed an underwater scene around it.

Photo Reference

1988
"GOLD MEDAL
MATCH"
OIL ON CANVAS

"Gold Medal Match" is a women's field hockey piece. It's another sport I knew very little about. It was educational to experience a wide variety of sports such as this.

"Match Sprint" is a painting from the Olympic Velodrome, an arena that was probably the most fun to watch an event in. The seats come right down to the track, so I was able to get positioned where I could almost reach out and touch the cyclists as they went by. The Velodrome was one place I could sketch without attracting a crowd.

SEOUL · 1988
OLYMPIC VELODROME

1988
"MATCH SPRINT"
OIL ON CANVAS

SEOUL OLYMPICS

1988

Photo Reference

1988
"FENCERS"
GRAPHITE

The Olympic experience was a test in many ways. In a city of ten million, one of the biggest challenges was finding ways to get from one stadium to another. Our guide helped us get about the city in his van, but I found that much more time was spent on trains, in taxis and in lots of traffic.

The fencing slides and sketch show how I typically do my research. In an afternoon spent at the fencing preliminaries, I used about four rolls of film, produced two or three sketches and had the material I needed.

"Butterfly" was painted before Seoul based on research I did at the U.S. training site in Colorado Springs. My hope was to capture the concentration of a swimmer in a competitive event.

1987
"BUTTERFLY"
OIL ON CANVAS

1992
"ICE DANCERS"
OIL ON CANVAS

WINTER OLYMPICS

"I ce Dancers" was done for the U.S. Olympic Committee as a painting that would be reproduced as a poster for the 1992 Winter Olympic Games. At the Summer Olympics, of course, you don't get to do much research for Winter Olympic events. I had an opportunity in 1990 to do artwork for the U.S. Olympic Festival in the Twin Cities and some of the winter events were there. It provided an opportunity to research the skating events.

1992
"PRACTICE ROUTINE"
OIL ON CANVAS

1992
"DOWNHILL"
OIL ON CANVAS

I have never been very interested in skiing myself, but I find it to be a great action sport to watch. In these two paintings, the effect of white snow is achieved by lifting out the oil pigment, leaving the muted whitish texture of snow. The flying snow is created by spattering opaque paint onto the canvas.

CALGARY / 1988

THE OLYMPIC TRADITION CONTINUES

Calgary 88

XV WINTER OLYMPICS
CALGARY CANADA

These are two different pieces that were done for the Calgary Olympics for ABC Television. These were painted ahead of the Games as sponsor give-aways. They gave me an opportunity to do some Winter Olympic canvases that I had not done before. These are generic athletes in typical winter scenes using the logos for Calgary that year.

1987
"ALPINE GOLD"
OIL ON CANVAS

1987
"WINNING FORM"
OIL ON CANVAS

BASKETBALL

I was fortunate to attend the University of North Carolina. I had been a basketball fan since before I graduated from high school in Cincinnati, where I saw a lot of basketball with my friends at the University of Cincinnati when Oscar Robertson was playing there.

When I got to UNC I had a basketball addiction, so I couldn't resist attending all the games and several of the practice sessions. The coach at that time was Frank McGuire, but he had an assistant named Dean Smith. I had the opportunity to interview Dean Smith when I was working for the campus newspaper, The Daily Tar Heel, for my friend Elliott Cooper, the sports editor at the time.

Elliott game me the opportunity to do both basketball and football writing, and I was the staff sports artist for three years. So I naturally was excited and pleased following the 1993 national championship that UNC won over Michigan, especially when I was asked to develop a painting to be produced as a limited-edition print to commemorate their national championship.

The painting depicts the senior leader of that team, George Lynch, shooting the ball, and in the background you can see Dean Smith and to his right assistant Bill Guthridge. This painting was a lot of fun to work on because of my interest in North Carolina. I suppose I'm destined to always be a Tar Heel addict when it comes to basketball and also the university in general.

1993
"NATIONAL
CHAMPIONS"
OIL ON CANVAS

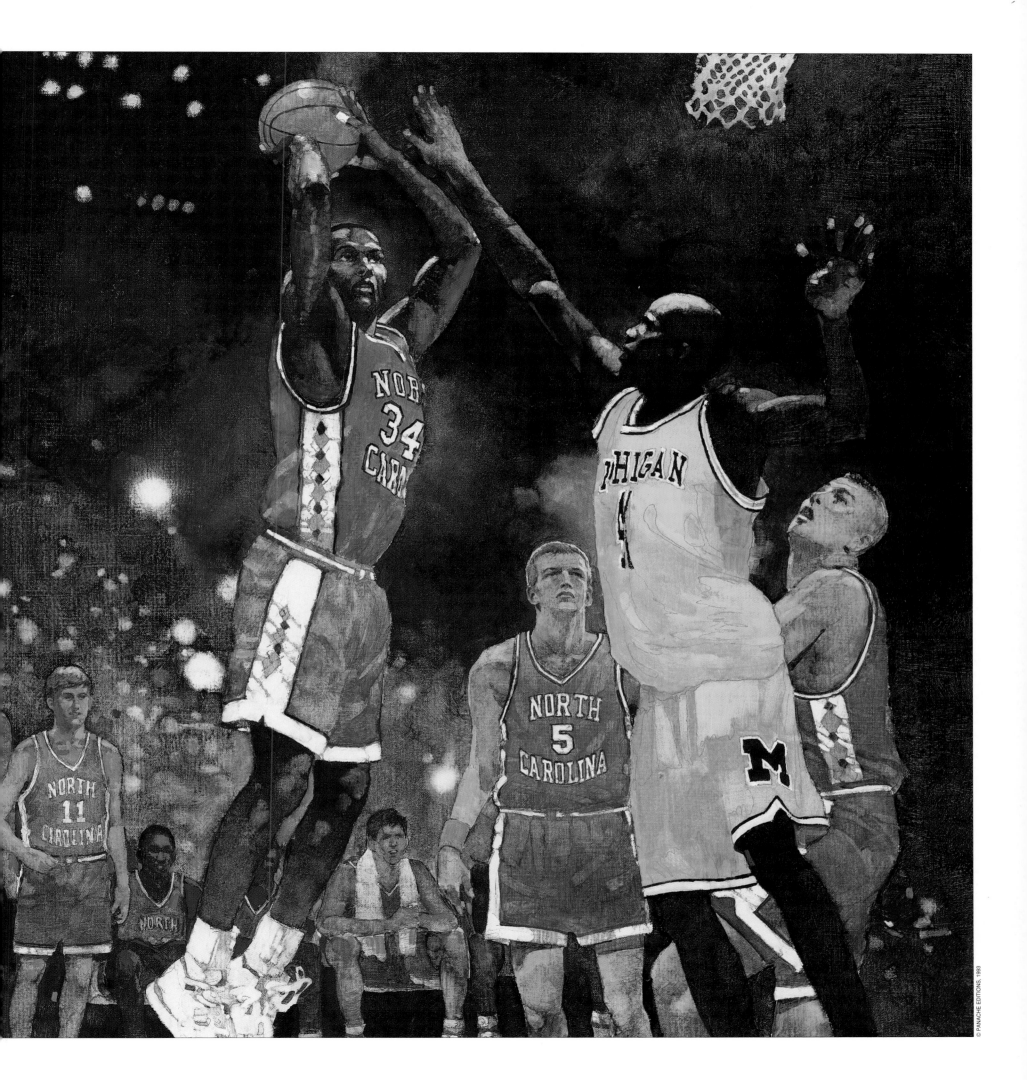

"MAGIC JOHNSON

IS A MAN WHO, IN MY MIND,

WILL ALWAYS BE KNOWN

AS A BASKETBALL PLAYER,

WHETHER HE'S ON

THE COURT OR NOT."

1992
"COURT OF DREAMS"
OIL ON CANVAS

1992
"LAST SECONDS"
OIL ON CANVAS

This is a sequence of paintings that I did for Sports Illustrated in 1992. The art director, Darrin Perry, asked me to develop some paintings to accompany a story about an NCAA tournament game between Kentucky and Duke the previous year. It was the game in which Christian Laettner took a pass with just 2.1 seconds on the clock and made a basket to win the game as time ran out. All that remained in the SI files was the videotape, so I had that plus slides of the players in other situations, and I was asked to develop these five paintings that show the sequence from the in-bounds pass from Grant Hill to the shot by Laettner.

1992
"THE SHOT HEARD
ROUND THE WORLD"
OIL ON CANVAS

David Robinson
USA Center   9.24.88   SEOUL
USA vs CHINA

1988
"DAVID ROBINSON"
GRAPHITE

This is a drawing of David Robinson in his Olympic uniform done in Seoul during the 1988 Olympics. David was also on the Dream Team in 1996, the Atlanta version of the Dream Team, which is shown in the painting at the right. That assignment involved doing a scene, with all the players visible, that I had to paint before the team had ever come together. This is an oil painting on canvas, probably about 30 inches by 40 inches. It is larger than the previous Dream Team painting and was developed from a variety of reference sources.

1996
"ATLANTA GOLD"
OIL ON CANVAS

1976
"JOHNNY UNITAS"
WATERCOLOR

FOOTBALL

My interest in football relates to my dad and me watching NFL games together on television on Sundays. But I didn't actually see professional football until I came to Dallas and had the opportunity to watch the Cowboys.

One day I got a call from David Boss, who was the creative director for NFL Properties in Los Angeles in the 1970s. He asked me to do a portfolio of paintings for an article in Pro magazine. That led to many assignments over a 10- or 12-year period.

This is Johnny Unitas, one of the 1970s Pro Bowl MVPs I did for the NFL. These are watercolors that combine not only a portrait of the player but also some sort of action in a montage setting. These show my fascination with sports in the earlier days.

It's a lot of good fortune that I've been able to do something that I really want to do. It's really the one thing I want to do. It's the only thing I'm cut out to do.

Being an artist isn't as easy as it might seem. It takes a lot of dedication to produce what I would consider good art. You're always striving to produce a great painting. I don't think I've ever produced a great painting, but I've tried to. I think my best work is ahead of me. I certainly hope it is. I'm always learning and trying to grow.

This is a portrait of Roger Staubach that I
did for the NFL in 1980. I really enjoyed
doing this portrait because of Roger being
a Dallas Cowboy and my living in Dallas. I always
pulled for the Dallas Cowboys. Sports is like hear-
ing a favorite song. I can see a player and I can
remember watching the game and who I watched
it with at the time. It evokes those kind of memories. And certainly, with Roger, I have a number
of memories like that.

I'm a jazz fan and I have been for a long time.
I like nothing more than putting on a Duke
Ellington or Pat Metheny CD. I'm inspired by that
because jazz is so improvisational. It tends to
grow and change, and that's how I work. I try to
learn from my mistakes and improvise occasion-
ally, inventing things and letting accidental things
happen that contribute to what I do.

1980
"ROGER STAUBACH"
WATERCOLOR

1981
"WALTER PAYTON"
WATERCOLOR

Among the early things I did for the NFL was the theme painting for Super Bowl IX in 1975 that was used on the tickets and posters. I did similar posters for the Pro Bowl as well.

I'm always experimenting. I think it's important for an artist to stretch himself in the work he does, to keep evolving and growing. It's dangerous to become static in art. If you become satisfied with what you're doing and essentially do the same painting over and over again, I don't think you're really doing art; you're simply copying yourself and really not growing as an artist.

SUPER BOWL IX

NEW ORLEANS, LOUISIANA
TULANE STADIUM

AFC VERSUS NFC FOR THE NFL CHAMPIONSHIP
AND THE VINCE LOMBARDI TROPHY

SUNDAY, JANUARY 12, 1975
2:00 P.M.

B. Forbes

1975
"SUPER BOWL IX"
WATERCOLOR

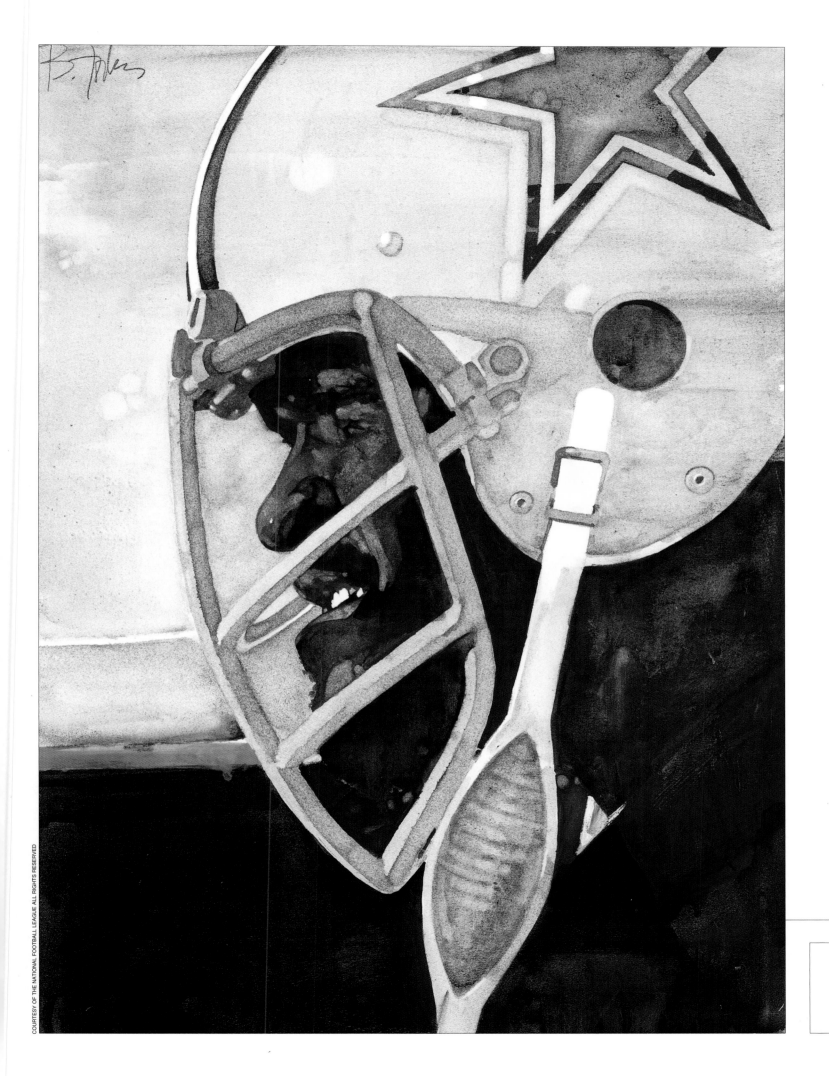

1974
"RAYFIELD WRIGHT"
WATERCOLOR

1989
"MANN IN PADS"
OIL ON CANVAS

This is a piece I did for a project for Southern Methodist University. When their football team came off probation from the death penalty (in the early '90s) they wanted a retrospective to honor some of their past great players. They had decided to play their games on-campus instead of in Texas Stadium, and they were trying to create some interest. It's unfortunate that this project was never completed, but the paintings I did as a result are some of my favorite works. Gerald Mann is the player here (at left), a lineman who played for them back in the '30s.

Pencil Sketch

1989
"DOAK"
OIL ON CANVAS

1989
"ERIC DICKERSON"
OIL ON CANVAS

This is a sketch I did for a group of paintings for Sports Illustrated. They were done as a sequence in the late '80s for an article about the legendary game between Stanford and Cal in which there was that three-lateral play that went the length of the field for a touchdown in the last few seconds. The last painting showed the player scoring a touchdown while going through the band, which had already come onto the field. The thing is, there were no photos. All SI had was a video. I was asked to develop 20 small paintings that would show the evolution of the play from the first lateral to the guy scoring the touchdown, all from video reference.

1984
"THE PLAY"
OIL ON CANVAS

1984
"THE BEAR"
OIL ON CANVAS

1984
"THE CARDINAL"
OIL ON CANVAS

In terms of procedure, typically what I'll do is develop two or three sketches in pencil for an assignment just to give me an idea of where I'm going with a piece. Frequently, especially if it's a large painting, I'll do little color thumbnails, maybe an inch wide. I'm not painting detail, I'm just trying different color schemes and different value studies so I can get a sense of how a painting is going to look.

At that size, you're strictly doing color and form. That helps me tremendously in developing a painting and keeping it simple.

Most of the color schemes I use tend to be fairly simple. I'm not all over the place. I try to select two or three primary colors. I work with a lot of earth tones. I try to keep the color schemes fairly simple so that I end up with something that's graphic and cleanly designed.

1979
"THE PRO BOWL"
WATERCOLOR

GOLF

This is the sport that I most enjoy playing, and I've played on a fairly regular basis for many years. My dad taught me how to play when I was about 12 or 13 years old. He showed me how to swing the club and is really the person that I would credit with giving me a good, basic golf swing. He taught me how to do it the right way from the beginning.

My dad encouraged me to play because it's a game that you can play your whole life. As long as you're able to swing the club and get around a little bit, it's a way to get outdoors and it's a great sport to enjoy. The only problem is, it's addictive.

The thing I like about golf from an artistic standpoint is that no two holes look the same. They all have their own character. Whether it's a course on the West Coast, the way it differs from a course in Florida or New England or Colorado . . . all golf courses in this country and the world have their own character and their own look.

For an artist, it gives me endless variety in the kind of work that I can do, whereas painting tennis or football or almost any other sport played in an arena that looks like almost any other arena can be a bit repetitive over a period of time.

It's hard to find new ways to show the same thing over and over again. Golf isn't like that, which makes it a great sport to paint, and to play.

1997
"GAMBLER'S
PARADISE"
OIL ON CANVAS

These two paintings are typical of the 10 paintings I've done for Peter Jacobsen's Fred Meyer Challenge in Portland, Ore., and are two of my particular favorites. Arnold Palmer has appeared in all 10 of the charity tournaments, as has Peter, each time playing with two of the other well-known pros.

I've painted Palmer so many times that I think I could probably do him without any reference material. He's certainly a golf legend, a great guy and someone I've enjoyed meeting.

1991
"PORTLAND
GOLF CLUB"
OIL ON CANVAS

1994
"THE OREGON
GOLF CLUB"
OIL ON CANVAS

Photo Reference

These are two paintings from The Pebble Beach National Pro-Am. The one above is the eighth fairway. I was asked to include Arnold Palmer, Jack Nicklaus, Clint Eastwood and Jack Lemmon. Eastwood and Lemmon are always two of the favorite amateurs in the tournament. In this case, when we finished the print and took it to Pebble Beach, we were able to get the four players to sign 100 of the prints.

At the signing, Clint Eastwood walked into the clubhouse and said hello and at the same time Jack Lemmon was just finishing a round and he came in. I pulled prints for the two of them while they signed and discussed scripts and actors and the biz that they're in. I found it very fascinating to watch two people that I had admired for many years on the screen talking among themselves about what they do just as I would to another artist about what I do.

1994
"THE LEGENDARY
7TH"
OIL ON CANVAS

ELEVEN IN A ROW ~ 1945 ◆ MIAMI FOUR BALL ◆

CANADIAN OPEN ◆

TAM O'SHANTER ◆

NELSON -6
SARAZEN -3

◆ PGA CHAMPIONSHIP ◆ CHICAGO VICTORY ◆ PHILADELPHIA

1995
"ELEVEN IN A ROW"
OIL ON CANVAS

This is a painting I did for the Byron Nelson Classic. The assignment was to depict Byron in a golf course setting to commemorate his 11 victories in a row 50 years earlier in 1945. I decided to do it by framing the painting with the names of the 11 tournaments that he won consecutively.

In the process of doing the painting, I had the opportunity to visit with Byron and his wife. He was a genuinely nice man. He approved the sketches and I'm told he was very pleased with the painting.

Pencil Sketch

1997
"SCOTLAND"
OIL ON CANVAS

Watercolor Sketches

This painting was based on what I saw on a trip I made to Scotland in 1997 to do some work for a resort called Skibo Castle. I had the opportunity to see a number of golf courses and to play the Carnegie course at Dornoch. The experience of playing golf in Scotland is wonderful. It's quite different from any of the golf courses in this country. It was very enjoyable.

This piece was done for a limited-edition print to give a view of what it's like to play golf in the heather — the fast-moving clouds, the frequent wind, the castles and water in the distance.

These paintings illustrate my interest in the early days of golf, even though one is a contemporary painting. The painting on the left is based on some photos I took of Payne Stewart in Portland while he was taking an approach shot to one of the greens. It's not really a portrait of Payne, but I've always felt that the knickers he wears contribute to the overall nostalgic feel of golf.

The above painting is based on an early photo of Gene Sarazen. Again, it's not really a portrait of Sarazen, but it gives the nostalgic feeling that that sort of wardrobe evokes about the history of golf and the early days of a classic sport.

Photo Reference

1995
"PALMER AT
GREYSTONE"
OIL ON CANVAS

Photo Reference

"PALMER IS A LOT OF FUN TO WORK WITH BECAUSE OF HIS CHARACTER AND INSTANTLY RECOGNIZABLE PHYSIQUE ON THE GOLF COURSE."

1998
"SAWGRASS"
OIL ON CANVAS

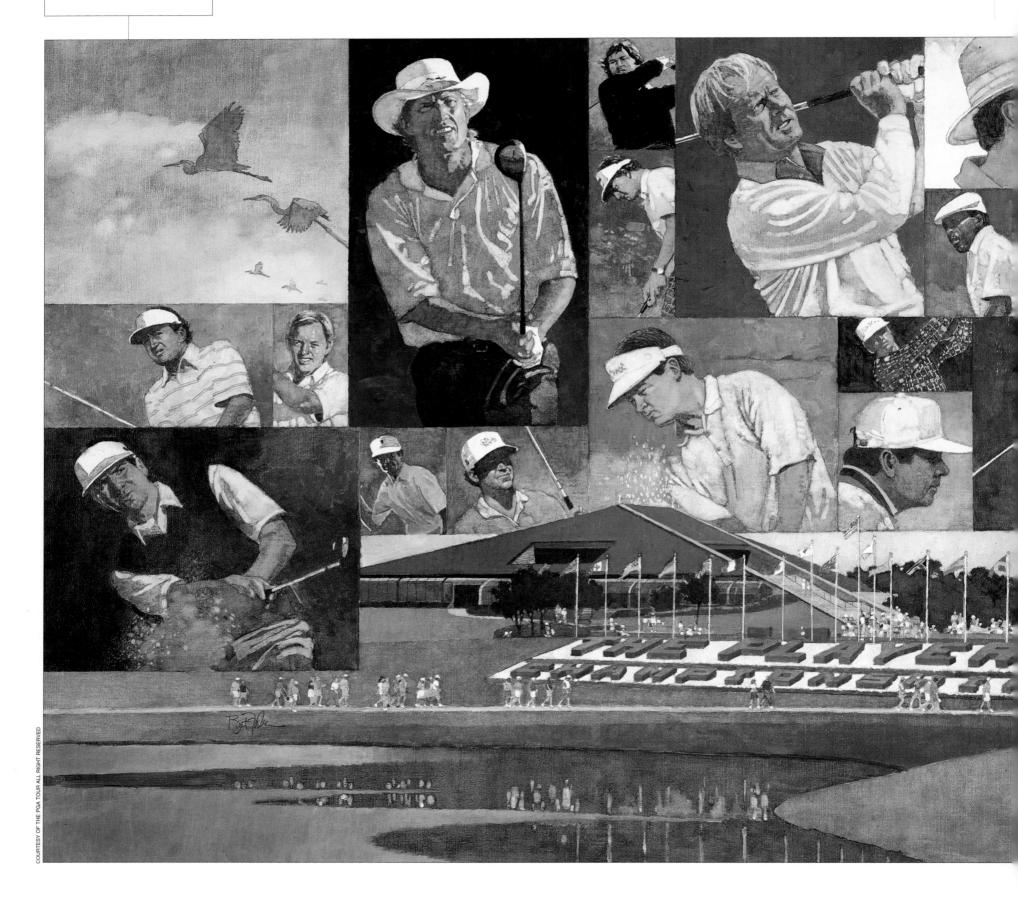

1998
"HOMESTEAD"
WATERCOLOR SKETCH

Pencil Sketch

Babe Didrickson

Tom Watson

Byron Nelson

Nancy Lopez

Bobby Locke

"Old Tom" Morris

Bobby Jones

Ben Hogan

Greg Norman

Chi Chi Rodriguez

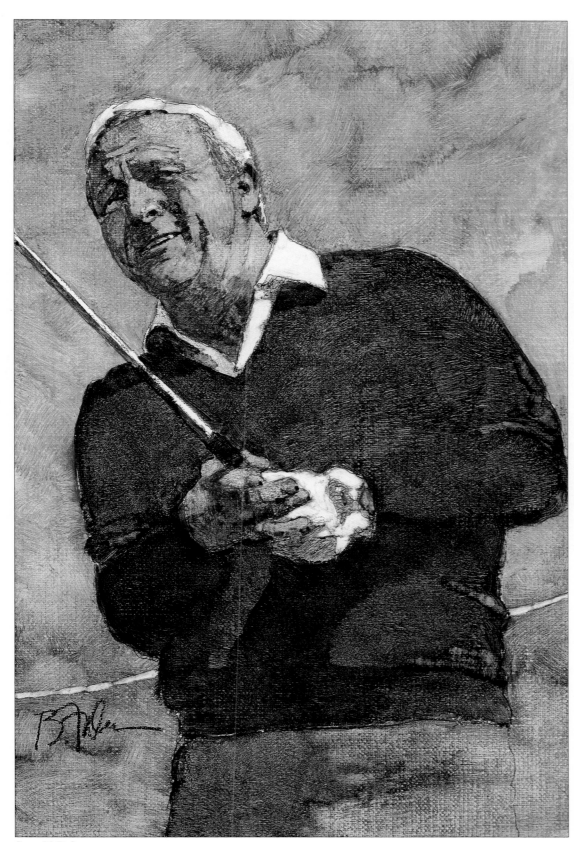

Arnold Palmer

1993
"GOLF CARD SET"
OIL ON CANVAS

Joyce Wethered

HAGLER VS HEARNS
4·15·85

1984
"HEARNS VS. HAGLER"
OIL ON CANVAS

The painting below comes from another Sports Illustrated story featuring Sugar Ray Leonard, another very colorful athlete for an artist to portray.

After doing numerous boxing paintings over the years, I felt almost qualified to coach the sport or become a referee, because I had learned so much about the strategy of a bout and how it might vary, depending on the fighters. So I guess painting really can be educational. I've learned something from every assignment that I've had.

1983
"SUGAR RAY"
WATERCOLOR

This is an Olympic piece done prior to the 1984 Olympics for Anheuser-Busch, part of a series of paintings I did for a poster and calendar promotion. This is based on references of Cassius Clay, later known as Muhammad Ali, in the ring during his Olympic year in 1960.

I still really don't enjoy boxing as much as baseball or golf because it's such a punishing sport and it can be painful to watch. People do get hurt, but as you study fighters and watch the training they go through, you realize that it takes an enormous amount of athletic ability, reflexes and timing to be a good fighter. It really is a skill that's learned, but they pay a heavy price, which we know when we see Ali today.

1984
"OLYMPIANS"
WATERCOLOR

STAMPS

I've enjoyed doing a number of stamps for the U.S. Postal Service, not all of which have been sports-oriented. I was originally asked to do a stamp on Kit Carson for a series that was subsequently canceled and never printed.

The first printed stamp I did was in 1984. It was an Abigail Adams commemorative stamp. It was not sports-oriented, but it got me into the stamp business and began a run of doing a number of stamps.

Doing art for the postal service is quite different than most assignments because of the reproduction size. Artists are required to do stamps in a format of roughly 5-by-7 inches. This can vary depending on the stamp, but generally it's a very small painting. For that reason, I always do them in watercolor because I can control the paint and the color at that size better than I can in oil.

The first sports assignment from the postal service was the 1988 Summer Olympics stamp. The assignment was pretty much what it tends to be for that sort of thing: to select a sport and a generic athlete to depict the Games. It's a little hard to do for something that's as diverse as the Olympics with so many different events. I decided to go with the gymnast on the rings.

The key here is to keep the design simple, graphic and colorful so that it will work at a reduced size.

1988
"SUMMER OLYMPICS"
WATERCOLOR

The one stamp that I've enjoyed creating more than any other was the one that honored New York Yankees legend Lou Gehrig. Being a baseball fan, I had always admired Gehrig and his accomplishments as a player.

The assignment required both a portrait and a full-figure image in the frame. I decided to use a baseball green for the background and incorporated the Yankees pinstripes as part of the design.

Before the stamp was issued, I was also asked to design a poster to help create awareness for the stamp. The original oil canvas used for the poster was later presented to President George Bush.

1989
"LOU GEHRIG"
OIL ON CANVAS

1989
"LOU GEHRIG"
WATERCOLOR

OLYMPIAN

USA
25

This is part of a series called The Olympians. Jesse Owens is probably the most well-known athlete in the series. You can see a couple of the sketches that I did, and then you can also see the stamp chosen by the committee that actually makes the decision on which stamps are used and which aren't.

Another requirement for postage stamps, when an artist is asked to do one, is that you're also asked to do the typeface design and the entire design of the stamp. In the case of all these stamps, I not only did the painting, but I designed and ordered the type for the title of the stamp and the "USA" wording and the amount of postage, and I decided the positioning for all that.

So, doing a stamp includes working with an image, selecting the type style and working the Olympic rings into it all. It becomes a design project as much as an illustration or painting project.

1990
"JESSE OWENS"
WATERCOLOR

1990
"HELENE MADISON"
WATERCOLOR

One of the neat things about doing a postage stamp was, at least back then, that they always invited the artist to attend the dedication ceremony of the stamp. The five Olympic stamps were dedicated in Minneapolis during the Olympic Festival that was held there. The trip there was a lot of fun because we had an opportunity to attend a lot of the Festival events and to meet Jesse Owens' daughter and family members of the other Olympians.

1990
"EDDIE EAGAN"
WATERCOLOR

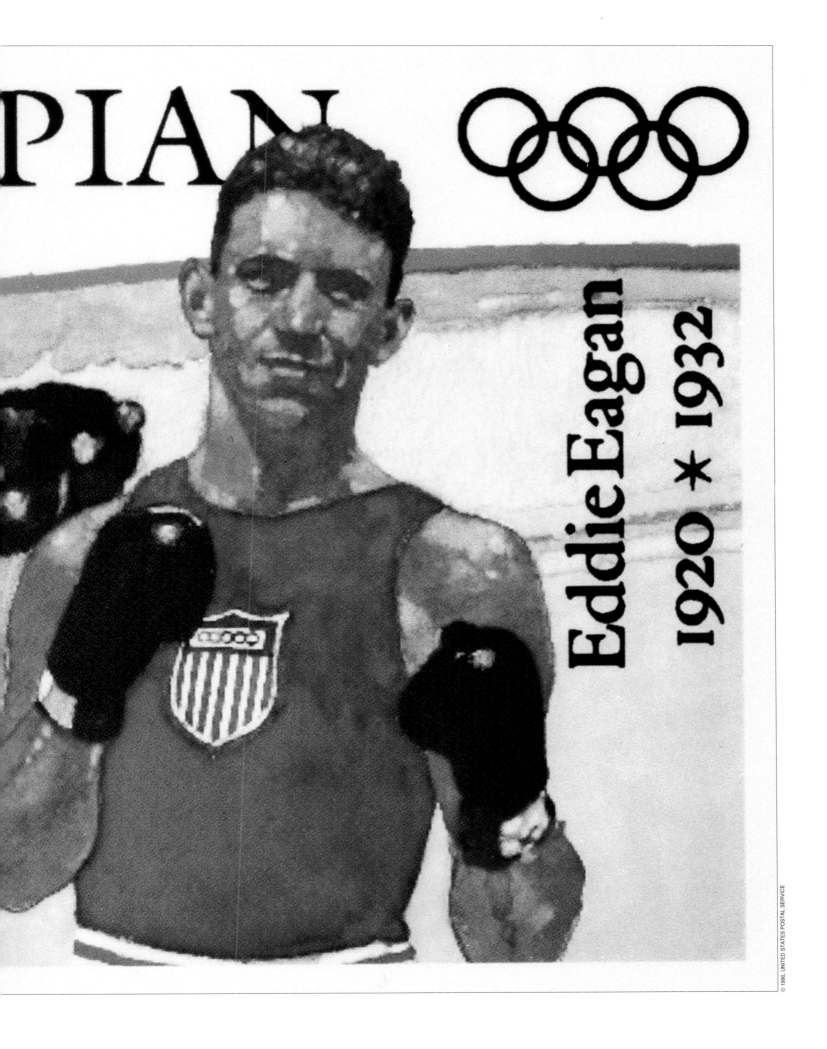

PIAN

Eddie Eagan
1920 ✳ 1932

1990
"OLYMPIANS"
WATERCOLOR

Boxer and bobsledder Eddie Eagan was the only U.S. gold medal winner in both the Summer and Winter Games.

EDDIE EAGAN
1920 · 1932

Swimmer Helene Madison won three Olympic gold medals in the Summer Games at Los Angeles in 1932.

HELENE MADISON
1932

Good art requires a lot of time and a lot of patience. Being an artist is not always as easy as it might seem. The ever-present deadlines and the pressure to always be your best can easily get in the way of concentrating on the painting itself and staying in touch with the personal side of your work.

I'm frequently asked what my favorite piece is, of all the paintings I've done. The answer for me is always "the next one." I'm never totally satisfied with any work, and I'm always striving to learn and improve what I do.

Talent is often the product of hard work, long hours, patience and dedication. All of us have talent in one area or another, but not everyone is willing to make the sacrifices it takes to build on it. I consider whatever ability I have to be a blessing from God. What I do with it is up to me.

OLYMPICS 88

22 USA

1988
"WINTER OLYMPICS"
WATERCOLOR

USA
22

1988 OLYMPICS

1988
"CALGARY"
WATERCOLOR

These are the Winter Olympics stamps I did for the U.S. in 1988, which is similar to the Summer Games stamp in that it's a case of selecting an event and a generic participant. It can't look like anybody. You have to be very careful when you're designing stamps that you don't use a model. Unless it's a portrait of a specific person, you're not allowed to have anybody that would be recognizable.

1991
"WINTER GAMES"
WATERCOLOR

Doing stamps has been a good experience for me. It gave me an opportunity to take my family to Cooperstown (for the dedication of the Gehrig stamp) for the first time. It was a wonderful experience. Cooperstown is one of my favorite places in the country. It's a small town and somewhere that the Baseball Hall of Fame just should be. It's proper.

The Olympics '92 stamps shown here are part of a five-stamp series featuring various winter events. The art here was again a design challenge as well as the challenge of developing paintings that work well as a group. I tried to make these watercolors more graphic and bold than the earlier Olympic stamps, which were more subtle in coloration. Reference material came from many sources, primarily the U.S. Olympic Committee files and my own skating photos.

1991
"WINTER GAMES"
WATERCOLOR

ETC

I've had the privilege to be commissioned to do work on numerous sports, from auto racing to marathons to sailing to fishing.

I was commissioned to do this piece by the Indianapolis Motor Speedway in 1995. It was used as a poster and program cover for the Indy 500. It's a nostalgic piece, a portrait of Wilbur Shaw in his Boyle Special from 1940. It's all a part of the legend of Indianapolis. I had the opportunity to go there and visit the track and shoot some reference photos and see a lot of the material that's housed in the Indianapolis museum inside the oval.

Actually, the car in the painting is now in the museum. It was fun to actually see a lot of the legendary cars and equipment and memorabilia.

For some of the larger paintings, I used little sketches as thumbnails for my own benefit to explore compositions in a very small and quick way.

For some of the others, I used the technique of painting in glazes. Some of my works are very much glaze paintings — there's no opaque paint in there. It's all done with turpentine and linseed oil and thinned washes of oil that are applied one over the other and sometimes rubbed back out with a towel or my fingers. I get my hands in my paintings a lot. It's just a technique I enjoy and am very comfortable with.

1995
"WILBUR SHAW"
OIL ON CANVAS

The first time I had the opportunity to work with the sport of sailing was during the 1988 Olympics in Korea. In 1991, I had another opportunity, this time to do poster paintings for the America's Cup races. Dennis Conner asked if I would come to San Diego to research and develop three paintings of Stars and Stripes, his entry in the 1992 America's Cup.

The first painting is the one to the right, called "Stars and Stripes." The next piece is called "The Challenge." All of these are large canvasses, which I needed to capture the scope of the sea and sails. Sailing is quite different from any other sport and requires a different perspective.

The paintings were reproduced as posters and displayed in San Diego.

1992
"STARS AND STRIPES"
OIL ON CANVAS

The small painting on the right was done as a study for another painting that I never produced. This one I particularly like and may yet develop into a larger piece. It's only about 4 inches high and is typical of the kind of sketches I do before beginning a large painting. Studies like this help me work out color schemes and value patterns without much detail involved. I might do a few of them just to make sure that I'm happy with the direction I'm taking.

1988
"HIGH NOON"
WATERCOLOR

1992
"THE CHALLENGE"
OIL ON CANVAS

Thense pieces are part of an ongoing series I've been working on since about 1990. They are purely personal and not intended for reproduction, although four of them have been made into posters. As I've said before, I enjoy working on nostalgic pieces that deal with the early, less-polished days of sport.

I decided to do these single features, standing in non-action poses, to allow me to improvise and try new things. I have used

family and friends as models and some, like the tennis player, I just made up without reference.

My good friend Ward Mayborn is the fisherman in "The Day's Catch," my daughter is the basis for the lady golfer and my son is the hunter.

There are eight of these in all and I am usually in the process of working on one at any given time. I take my time and develop them as I see fit. The golfer on Page 1 was the first in this series.

1995
"THE DAY'S CATCH"
OIL ON CANVAS

1990
"LADY GOLFER"
OIL ON CANVAS

1983
"GOOD CATCH"
WATERCOLOR

This is another work done between boxing assignments for Sports Illustrated. This was quite different: a story about ice fishing in Michigan. Since it was actually to be done in the summer, it would have done me little good to go to Michigan to do my research. So I put together research from a wide variety of sources and actually made up some things.

The horse team is based on a photograph from the Library of Congress, actually, of a man plowing a field with these two horses. I changed the color of the horses and added an ice landscape and snow and . . . presto — we've got ice fishing in Michigan.

1983
"ICE SLED"
WATERCOLOR

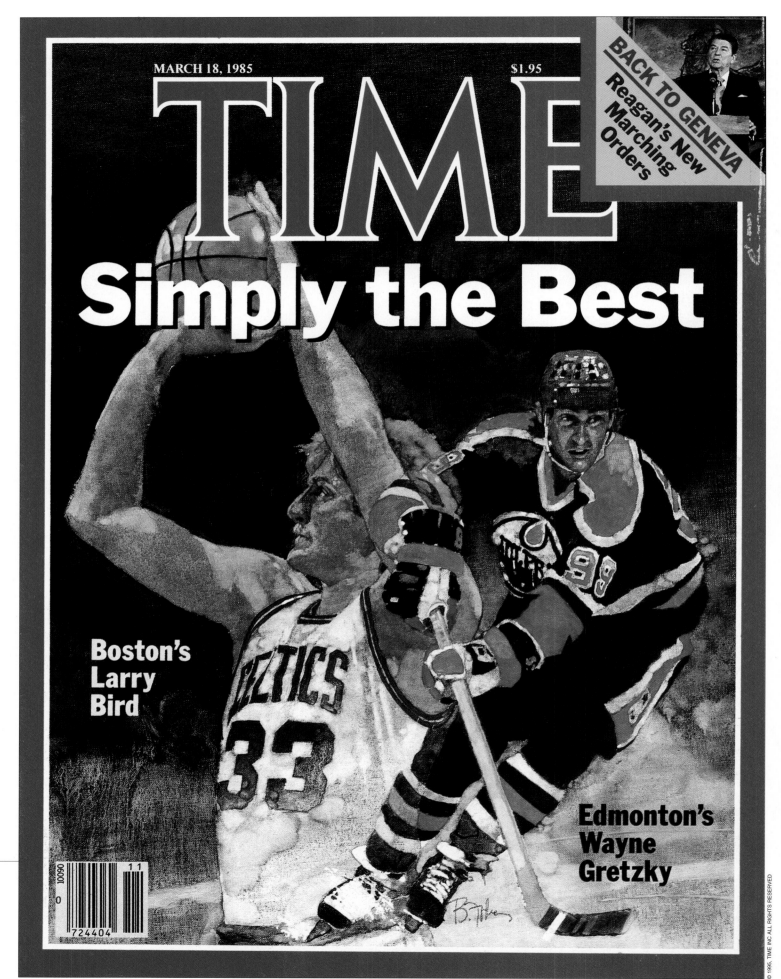

MARCH 18, 1985 $1.95

TIME

Simply the Best

Boston's
Larry
Bird

Edmonton's
Wayne
Gretzky

1985
"SIMPLY THE BEST"
OIL ON CANVAS

1987
"FACING OFF"
OIL ON CANVAS

The painting on the left is obviously a Time magazine cover. I was asked to do a painting that would combine portraits of Larry Bird and Wayne Gretzky for a story about those two athletes. When you work for Time magazine, there's always the potential that your work may never appear on the cover.

Being a news magazine, if a news event that is really cover-worthy takes place prior to that issue coming out, it will go on the cover and yours will be left by the wayside.

I really didn't think this particular cover would run because the Russian president (Konstantin Chernenko) was very near death. When I was in the Time office they showed me three different portraits of him, one of which would have run on the cover had he died that week in 1985. They asked me to do this painting as a backup piece. So I did the painting in about three days and kept watching the news. The president's death was about two days after the deadline, so I barely made the cover.

1996
"WHITE ROCK
MARATHON"
OIL ON CANVAS

These are two marathon paintings, both done for posters. The Boston Marathon piece is interesting in that I took artistic license here. If these runners were actually running where they are, with Old Ironsides in the background, they'd be running on the water. But with art, anything is possible. I decided to stage it this way because I wanted to feature Old Ironsides and the Bunker Hill monument in the background because they're recognizable Boston landmarks. In a painting you can create whatever you want to. The people in Boston didn't complain, I thought the painting looked good, so I guess it worked.

With the other piece, this park doesn't really look quite this leafy when the race is run (in Dallas) in late November. But it looks better to have the trees in full leaf.

1992
"BOSTON
MARATHON"
OIL ON CANVAS

Photo Reference

I did this as a personal painting prior to the 1988 Olympics. It became a painting that was produced as a poster, and it's a watercolor that shows a technique I've used a number of times. It's a process of subtraction that involves using watercolor washes on a hot-press board and then going back into those washes with a brush and lifting out color instead of adding color on the top.

It creates an interesting effect. It allows the pattern of the shadows to become an integral part of the composition rather than an afterthought. It becomes almost as important as the cyclists themselves. It's just an interesting way of working. It allows you to suggest areas of negative space that really complement and add a certain subtlety to a painting.

1987
"THE SPRINT"
WATERCOLOR

1978
"STEVE CAUTHEN"
WATERCOLOR

On the left is a painting I did several years ago for Sports Illustrated, one of the very first things I did for them. This is jockey Steve Cauthen, who was very famous in the late '70s.

The other painting was originally done for a racetrack in New York state. I wasn't happy with the color on the original painting, so I went back over the top and made changes. Sometimes I overwork paintings, but this one I thought benefited from an extra stroke or two.

1994
"BY A NOSE"
OIL ON CANVAS

1987
"LUCKY HAT"
OIL ON CANVAS

"THERE'S SOMETHING VERY PEACEFUL AND NOSTALGIC ABOUT FISHING. IT'S SORT OF AN ACTIVITY THAT SEEMS FROZEN IN TIME."

1984
"JUBILATION"
WATERCOLOR